D1403560

THE
BRITISH
MUSEUM Pocket Dictionary

PHARAOHS
AND QUEENS

Marcel Marée

THE BRITISH MUSEUM PRESS

© 2005 The Trustees of the British Museum

Marcel Marée has asserted his right to be identified as the author of this work.

First published in 2005 by
The British Museum Press
A division of The British Museum
Company Ltd
46 Bloomsbury Street,
London, WC1B 3QQ

A catalogue record for this title is available from the British Library.

ISBN-13:   978-0-7141-3109-2
ISBN-10:   0-7141-3109-1

Designed and typeset by
HERRING BONE DESIGN.
Cover design by Proof Books.
Hieroglyphs typeset by Marcel Marée using Visual Glyph, a program developed by Günther Lapp.
Printed in Singapore.

All photographs are taken by the British Museum Photography and Imaging Dept, © The Trustees of the British Museum, except for the following.
Marcel Marée pp 10 bottom, 11, 19 bottom, 27 right, 38, 39, bottom.
Delia Pemberton p. 13
Werner Forman Archive pp 14, 43.

CONTENTS

A-Z Index of Kings & Queens

Egyptian Kingship

Many monuments from ancient Egypt record the names and deeds of its pharaohs and queens. Who were these people and what were their achievements?

The word 'pharaoh' comes from Egyptian *per-aa*, which means 'Great House'. This first referred to the royal palace but eventually to the king himself. Egyptians thought their pharaoh was half human, half divine. He was a manifestation of the falcon-god Horus. As the sun-cult grew important, the king was also seen as the son of Ra, the sun-god. These claims were expressed in the ruler's royal titles, which ultimately included five names with epithets (special titles). The throne- and birth-name became the most commonly used and were written in hieroglyphs inside oval 'cartouches'. Queens used cartouches as well, and this book includes the cartouches of the kings and queens it describes.

Lintel from a temple of Amenemhat III for the crocodile-god Sobek. The cartouche in the middle gives his birth-name, and the falcons stand over his Horus-name.

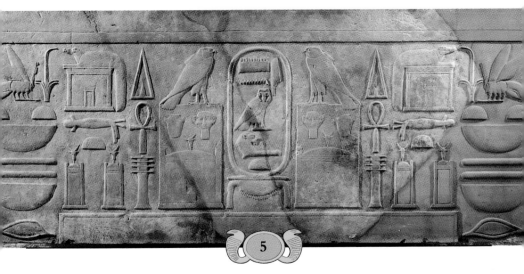

The king's task was to maintain *maat*, the divine order of justice and cosmic harmony. He was expected to 'create' temples and statues for the gods to live in. He had to maintain religious services, because the gods needed to be fed, washed and dressed each day. In theory, because he was half-divine, only the king could mediate between humankind and the gods. In practice, priests throughout the country performed the temple rituals on his behalf.

The king had to rule over a united country including both Upper and Lower Egypt (the Nile Valley and Delta), which in Egyptian tradition had once been separate kingdoms. Special crowns represented Upper and Lower Egypt, or were a combination of both. The king's throne-name was written with epithets such as 'King of Upper and Lower Egypt' or 'Lord of the Two Lands'. He also had to defend the realm from chaos across its borders. Pharaoh is often shown slaying foreigners, even if he did not actually fight any wars. Genuine accounts of war are illustrated with scenes of defeated peoples paying tribute and respect.

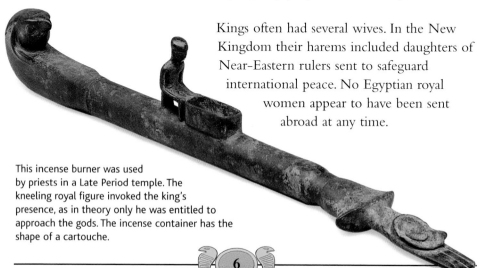

Kings often had several wives. In the New Kingdom their harems included daughters of Near-Eastern rulers sent to safeguard international peace. No Egyptian royal women appear to have been sent abroad at any time.

This incense burner was used by priests in a Late Period temple. The kneeling royal figure invoked the king's presence, as in theory only he was entitled to approach the gods. The incense container has the shape of a cartouche.

Usually, the king's heir apparent was his eldest son by his principal queen. Often this 'Great Royal Wife' must have helped shape her husband's policies, but Egyptian accounts never record this. Some of the most influential queens are shown in monuments beside the king, but normally on a smaller scale. Occasionally a widowed queen would act as regent for an underage new king, but queens were not expected to rule independently. The few queens who did rule alone are left out of later historical records.

In ancient Egypt, monuments always present kings and their deeds in an idealised way, doing the things expected of them. The visual arts offer no lifelike portraits. They uphold an image of youthful, energetic kings and graceful, loyal queens. Therefore, it is hard to grasp the personalities of even the most famous Egyptian royal figures. The following pages present the main facts that we know about them.

List of Egyptian kings, from the temple of Ramesses II at Abydos. Ruling queens and certain kings are deliberately omitted.

1st–2nd Dynasties (3100–2686 BC)

Narmer   Aha   Den   Peribsen   Khasekhemwy

In late prehistoric times, Egypt had developed a high level of cultural sophistication and political organisation.

A number of kings from the end of this period are recorded at Upper Egyptian sites such as Abydos and Hierakonpolis. It seems likely that some of them – the last being Narmer – already controlled the whole of Egypt. It is doubtful whether Upper and Lower Egypt ever were two rival kingdoms, as later traditions would have it. King Narmer was succeeded by Aha. Evidence suggests that he was the founder of the capital city of Memphis. Later sources call him Menes. The invention of the hieroglyphic script helped the country to develop a centralised administration.

Fragment of ivory plaque with the name of Narmer.

The kings of the 1st Dynasty, and the last two of the 2nd, were buried in the desert at Abydos. The early 2nd Dynasty kings were the first to be buried at Saqqara. It seems that the royal tombs had square superstructures filled with sand and gravel, so-called *mastabas*. Associated 'funerary enclosures' for ceremonial

Ivory label showing king Den smiting an Asian foe.

purposes have been found in Abydos near the edge of the cultivated land. Building in brick was the norm, but the tomb of king Den is the earliest with surviving elements of stone; part of its substructure is built of granite.

The late 2nd Dynasty was a period of conflict between rival political or religious factions. King Peribsen first had a name that linked him with the god Horus, but he changed this to a Seth-name. In Egyptian myth, the god Seth fought against Horus for the throne of Egypt. Peribsen was apparently opposed by a king with the Horus-name Khasekhem ('The Power has appeared'). The latter then changed his name to Khasekhemwy ('The *Two* Powers have appeared'), which in writing is surmounted by both the Horus-falcon and the Seth-animal. This suggests he brought the conflict to an end. Khasekhemwy was the last ruler of the 2nd Dynasty, but the next two kings were related through his queen.

Stela (gravestone) of Peribsen from his tomb at Abydos. The Seth-animal above his name was later erased.

Djoser (2667-2648 BC)

Djoser was the second ruler of the 3rd Dynasty. His reign began a new era of great technical achievements. The world's earliest great stone buildings were constructed for this king.

Rows of faience tiles decorated the walls in Djoser's pyramid, in imitation of reed mats.

In Saqqara, Djoser's brilliant architect Imhotep created for him the first, stepped pyramid. It replaced the rectangular mud-brick structures (*mastabas*) that marked his predecessors' graves. The pyramid is surrounded by dummy palaces, shrines and a huge square intended as an eternal residence, complete with facilities for the king's jubilee festivals. The pyramid and a symbolic 'South Tomb' have wall reliefs that show Djoser forever performing his rejuvenating jubilees. On the north side of the pyramid, a large seated statue of the king was walled into a chamber with eye-holes, allowing his soul to receive the offerings presented there. The pyramid complex has an enormous enclosure wall with recesses imitating a palace façade. This evolved from the 'funerary enclosures' of earlier kings. Later 3rd-Dynasty kings all commissioned step pyramids, but none was completed.

Djoser's step pyramid towers over other buildings mimicking his palaces with associated jubilee courts and chapels. Brick and perishable materials have been translated into stone to last forever.

Sneferu (2613-2589 BC)

Sneferu founded the 4th Dynasty. His father, Huni, was the last king of the 3rd Dynasty, and his mother probably a minor wife.

Sneferu launched a campaign against Nubia and established a colony at Buhen to facilitate trade and mining activities. From Byblos (Lebanon) he obtained cedar to build large new ships. Quarrying expeditions exploited turquoise and copper mines in Sinai.

Sneferu built the first true pyramids. At Meidum he began with a step pyramid but late in his reign filled up its steps. By then, Sneferu had built two other smooth pyramids in Dahshur. The earliest of these started sinking when half-complete. The builders reduced the slope, creating a 'Bent Pyramid', and nearby constructed the 'Red' pyramid with a gentler slope from the outset. Sneferu was probably buried in the Red Pyramid. He also established what became the standard layout of a pyramid complex, including a satellite pyramid, a mortuary temple and a causeway to a 'valley temple' near the cultivated land.

Sneferu was remembered as an exemplary king. In the Middle Kingdom he was deified at his pyramid sites and in Sinai.

The 'Bent Pyramid' of Sneferu at Dahshur.

Khufu (2589-2566 BC)

 The best-known ruler of the 4th Dynasty is Sneferu's son and successor Khufu (Cheops). At Giza he built Egypt's largest pyramid, which once stood 146 m high.

As the pyramid was built, plans for its interior changed twice. Finally a burial chamber was completed high in the masonry. It now holds only an empty sarcophagus, but exquisite burial equipment was found in his mother's tomb near the pyramid. Smaller pyramids were constructed for Khufu's queens. Six giant pits carved into the desert floor held wooden ships – two of which have survived – for Khufu's travels in the Afterlife. The *mastaba* tombs of the king's officials lie rigidly arranged around the pyramid, reflecting Khufu's supreme authority as the head of a highly centralised state.

Little of Khufu's reign is documented, apart from some quarrying expeditions. The only known representation of him is a small ivory figure from Abydos. Later sources say he was a tyrant, but perhaps this was only because he built such a colossal tomb.

Granite block with the Horus-name of Khufu found in Bubastis, in the Delta.

Khafra (2558-2532 BC)

Khafra, the son of Khufu, became king after the short reign of his half-brother Djedefra. He built the second largest pyramid of Egypt, a short distance from his father's.

The pyramid's valley temple, with pillars and walls of granite from Aswan, housed magnificent royal statues. The finest shows Khafra enthroned with Horus as a falcon spreading its wings behind his head. The stone from which it is carved comes from a quarry in the western desert of Lower Nubia.

Khafra's most famous monument is the Great Sphinx, situated along the causeway that leads to his pyramid. This 73 metre-long lion with the king's head was carved from a rock knoll first quarried for pyramid blocks. The sphinx and its nearby temple had connections with the sun. A growing interest in the sun cult is also shown by the royal epithet 'son of Ra', first used by Djedefra and Khafra. In the New Kingdom the sphinx was worshipped as an image of the sun-god Horemakhet ('Horus in the Horizon').

The Great Sphinx with the face of Khafra, wearing the royal headcloth. The pyramid of Khufu is visible in the background.

13

Unas (2375-2345 BC)

Unas was the last ruler of the 5th Dynasty. Wall-reliefs from his pyramid complex at Saqqara include scenes of people struck by famine. These may show the beginning of the climate changes and drought that possibly contributed to the end of the Old Kingdom.

The earlier kings of the 5th Dynasty no longer built large pyramids, and the pyramid of Unas is the smallest of the Old Kingdom. However, the walls of its burial chambers are the first to be inscribed with a selection of the so-called Pyramid Texts. These are funerary spells intended to aid the king's resurrection and reunion with the gods in the Afterlife. These texts must originally have been provided on papyrus rolls or recited at the funeral. Parts of the texts use archaic language and must date back many centuries before Unas lived.

Inside the pyramid of Unas, the walls are covered with the earliest record of the 'Pyramid Texts'.

Pepi II (2278-2184 BC)

The last important king of the Old Kingdom, Pepi II, was only six when he inherited the throne. Statues from his early reign show him as a naked child or seated on the lap of his regent-mother. Tradition gives Pepi II a reign of 94 years, but surviving records from his own time only confirm 66 years.

At this time, a governor of Aswan called Harkhuf led a series of trade missions to a southern land called Yam, probably centred around Kerma in modern Sudan. A rare glimpse of the king's personality is recorded in a letter from the child-king that survived in Harkhuf's tomb. Harkhuf brought back a pygmy, which the young Pepi valued more highly than all the exotic trade goods. Pepi exresses his excitement and longing to see the pygmy.

In the course of Pepi's over-long reign, his grip on the country weakened. Provincial governments became hereditary and turned into virtually independent political entities. Pepi probably outlived his designated heirs and there was a power vacuum after his death. The 6th Dynasty (and Old Kingdom) soon ended with the brief reign of a female pharaoh, Nitiqret.

Calcite oil jar with the titles of Pepi II, including his Horus- and throne-name.

Mentuhotep II (2055-2004 BC)

King Mentuhotep II ended a period of political disintegration and began a new great epoch: the Middle Kingdom.

A time of political decline with no important rulers had followed the end of the 6th Dynasty – the First Intermediate Period. The short-lived kings of the 7th and 8th Dynasty, still ruling from Memphis, had only in name controlled the entire land. Then a line of rulers from Herakleopolis (the 9th-10th Dynasties) took over while a rivalling Dynasty (the 11th) emerged in Thebes, and Mentuhotep belonged to the latter. Armed conflicts became a regular occurrence. Mentuhotep II eventually pushed north and defeated the northern king.

After the country was reunited, Mentuhotep continued to rule from Thebes. He encouraged a revival of artistic production. His most famous building is his terraced funerary temple at Deir el-Bahari, on the Theban West Bank, where he and his queens were also buried. Two further kings called Mentuhotep ruled over Egypt until a vizier came to the throne as Amenemhat I, founding the 12th Dynasty.

Head of a statue of Mentuhotep II from his temple at Deir el-Bahari.

Senusret I (1965-1920 BC)

Amenemhat I was apparently murdered in a palace conspiracy. His son and designated successor, Senusret I, was out campaigning against the Libyans, but he managed to secure the throne for himself.

Amenemhat had moved the capital from Thebes back to the area of Memphis, where he founded a city called Itjtawy. His pyramid there – the first since the end of the Old Kingdom – was completed by Senusret I, who built his own nearby. Senusret strengthened his government and bound to him the powerful governors in Middle and southern Egypt.

On this stela from Elephantine, Senusret I is represented by his Horus-name. He receives life from the ram-headed god Khnum (extending the *ankh*-sign) and the goddess Satet.

Senusret had important military successes in Lower Nubia, where he built many fortresses extending to Buhen. Garrisons held the Nubian population in check, preventing any threat to Egypt's border, trade routes and gold-mining activities.

The arts reached exceptional heights in Senusret's reign and he built superbly decorated temples. In Heliopolis, he erected the earliest documented pair of obelisks, one of which is still in place.

Senusret III (1874-1855 BC)

The late-12th Dynasty king Senusret III drastically reformed the country's administration and pursued a vigorous foreign policy.

Senusret III put a stop to the extraordinary independence of some provincial governors. He took away their hereditary positions and created a rapidly growing bureaucracy. The nation was divided into a few administrative districts overseen by the king's viziers, who were only subordinate to the king himself.

Through four campaigns in Nubia, Senusret pushed the Egyptian border forward and extended the chain of fortresses to Semna. He curbed the growing political influence of Kush further south. Senusret's grip on Lower Nubia was so total that he came to be locally worshipped as a god. He also led a campaign into Palestine.

Statues of Senusret III show a radical new style. The traditional youthful appearance, already abandoned by his predecessor Senusret II, made way for aged, haggard features suggesting mature wisdom and burdening concern. This new form of idealisation was to dominate Egyptian art right up to the beginning of the New Kingdom.

Statue of Senusret III from the temple of Mentuhotep II at Deir el-Bahari, which he refurbished.

Amenemhat III (1855-1808 BC)

The reign of Senusret III's successor was long and peaceful. The earlier conquests in Nubia and a lively trade with Syria-Palestine brought great wealth. Amenemhat III spent lavishly on building and irrigation works.

Numerous quarrying expeditions took place around Egypt and in Sinai. In the Fayum oasis, large areas of marsh were drained to create new farmland. It became one of the country's most prosperous regions.

Head of a colossal statue of Amenemhat III.

Amenemhat built his most impressive monuments there, mostly dedicated to the crocodile god Sobek. At Biahmu, the king erected two colossal seated statues overlooking Lake Moeris. Originally Amenemhat was meant to be buried in a pyramid at Dahshur, but this was abandoned for another at Hawara. Next to the Hawara pyramid, a vast temple arose with so many rooms that later Classical authors called it 'the Labyrinth'. Fayum residents from the Graeco-Roman period worshipped Amenemhat as a god.

The king's pyramid at Hawara. An expanse of debris with fragments of columns marks the place where once 'the Labyrinth' stood.

13th–14th Dynasties (1795–1650 BC)

Neferhotep I   *Sobekhotep IV*

After the death of Amenemhat III, the 12th Dynasty came to an end with the short reigns of Amenemhat IV and queen Nofrusobek – a female pharaoh for lack of male heirs. From then the throne was claimed by a rapid succession of kings.

The kings of the so-called 13th Dynasty, still residing at Itjtawy, came from many different families. The majority only had brief reigns and achieved very little. There was still some building and mining activity, but no more expeditions went to Sinai. The burials of most of these kings, probably around Memphis, have not yet been found.

Control of Egypt's borders slackened. The Egyptian fortresses in Nubia still operated under the brother-kings Neferhotep I and Sobekhotep IV, the most important rulers of the 13th Dynasty. But soon after, Egyptian control of Nubia slipped, and the fortresses were conquered by the kingdom of Kush (modern Sudan). The eastern Delta was entered by people from Syria-Palestine, who settled in large communities, preserving their own culture. The rise in this region of the 14th Dynasty began an era of political fragmentation called the Second Intermediate Period.

Statue of Mentuhotep VI, one of the numerous short-lived kings of the 13th Dynasty.

The Hyksos (1650–1550 BC)

Khyan　*Apepi*

In the Delta, the 14th Dynasty was replaced by the 15th – how the two dynasties are related is not clear. The new kings originally came from Canaan and were known as 'rulers of foreign lands' (*Hyksos*). Their capital town was Avaris.

The Hyksos took Memphis and ended the Egyptian 13th Dynasty. They also took control of much of Middle Egypt. Kings Khyan and Apepi (Apophis) even held the south for some time. Native Egyptian rulers based at Thebes struggled for their independence.

The religious practices and material culture of the Hyksos demonstrate their foreign origin, but they also showed devotion to the Egyptian gods. They especially worshipped Seth, who resembled their own god Baal. The Hyksos rulers adopted the titles of pharaohs, using cartouches and throne-names in honour of Ra. They left few memorials; they mostly put their names on monuments of earlier Egyptian kings. The Hyksos introduced to Egypt new weapons and the military use of horses with chariots.

During the reign of king Apepi, the Thebans gathered enough strength to attack the Hyksos and ended the foreign occupation.

This lion statue was originally a human-headed sphinx of a 12th-Dynasty king. It was usurped and turned into a full lion for the Hyksos king Khyan.

16th–17th Dynasties (1650–1550 BC)

Taa   *Kamose*

The native Egyptian 16th and 17th Dynasties ruled at Thebes, while the northern half of Egypt was governed by the Hyksos.

For a time, the Hyksos also controlled southern Egypt. This probably ended the 16th Dynasty. However, the Hyksos failed to keep their hold on the south, and Thebes regained a fragile independence. The 17th Dynasty gathered strength to tackle the Hyksos. It also had to face invasions from the south by plundering armies from Kush, now a powerful kingdom which had already seized Egypt's former possessions in Lower Nubia. The Kushite kings were buried in vast tumulus tombs at Kerma, equipped with looted Egyptian objects.

At least one Theban king, named Taa, died in battle against the Hyksos. But his successor Kamose had more success. He re-established Egyptian control of Lower Nubia. Once he was safe from attack by the Kushites, he invaded the Hyksos territory and reconquered a large part of Middle Egypt.

The Theban kings of the Second Intermediate Period were buried on the capital's West Bank, at Dra Abu el-Naga. Here were found the gilded coffin of Intef VII and the heart scarab of Sobekemsaf II, two kings of the 17th Dynasty.

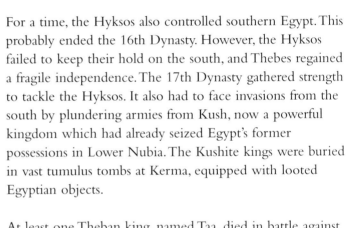

Ahmose (1550–1525 BC)

Ahmose, son of king Taa, was the founder of the 18th Dynasty and the New Kingdom. He completed the military campaigns against the Hyksos begun by Taa and Kamose. Victory came when Ahmose was only 20 years old.

Ahmose expelled the Hyksos from Egypt. He pursued and crushed them in campaigns in Syria-Palestine. Ahmose also strengthened Egyptian control of Lower Nubia. In the stronghold of Buhen, he installed a commander who became the first Viceroy of Kush – a special governor for Nubia. Egypt, now reunited and strong, began to trade again with most of the known world. Ahmose also oversaw major changes to the country's internal administration. He gave important positions to provincial governors who had helped him in his victorious campaigns.

Ahmose died at about 35 and was buried at Dra Abu el-Naga, in western Thebes. After his death he was worshipped as a god at Abydos until the late New Kingdom.

32191.

This rare portrait of Ahmose is the oldest surviving royal *shabti* (a small tomb figure meant to work for its owner in the Afterlife).

Ahmose Nefertari

 Queen Ahmose Nefertari was the sister and wife of king Ahmose, and the mother of his successor Amenhotep I. She was one of Egypt's most prominent queens.

Ahmose Nefertari was closely involved in the nation's religious organisation and she influenced the quarrying and building activities required for new temples. She played an important role in the cult of the god Amun, who became the national god as patron of the Theban kings. The queen was the first to hold the title of 'God's Wife' in Amun-Ra's temple at Karnak.

The queen outlived her husband and was regent for Amenhotep I during the early part of his reign. Her son also died before her and Ahmose Nefertari lived some time into the reign of Thutmose I.

The queen and Amenhotep I were both worshipped as patron deities of the West Bank at Thebes, where they established a community of workmen responsible for the royal tombs of the New Kingdom.

Painted figure of Ahmose Nefertari from a Ramesside tomb. Her black skin stands for rebirth after death, recalling her role as patron of the Theban cemeteries.

Amenhotep I (1525–1504 BC)

Amenhotep I was the son of Ahmose and Ahmose Nefertari. He was still young when he became king, and at first his mother acted as regent.

Amenhotep followed in his father's footsteps with military campaigns both in the Near East and in Nubia, and he further secured Egypt's political recovery. Building activity increased, especially at Thebes for the cult of the national god Amun-Ra. The high standards of artistic production achieved during the Middle Kingdom were restored under Amenhotep I.

Amenhotep's mortuary temple at Deir el-Bahari was later demolished by queen Hatshepsut to make room for her own, but the statues that adorned it have partly survived. Amenhotep's tomb was probably at Dra Abu el-Naga. His mummy was found in a 21st Dynasty cache at Deir el-Bahari along with other kings, reburied there to protect them from tomb robbers. As joint founder of a Theban community of artists, Amenhotep I was deified after his death.

One of the statues of Amenhotep I from his mortuary temple at Deir el-Bahari.

Thutmose I (1504–1492 BC)

 This king was of non-royal descent. How he came to the throne is not clear. He was a highly successful warrior, invading territories never reached by Egyptian armies before.

In three campaigns, Thutmose extended Egypt's military might as far north as the kingdom of Mitanni across the Euphrates, and in Nubia as far south as Kurgus, upstream from the fourth Nile cataract. Important trade routes came under secure Egyptian control. War spoils and tribute further boosted the economy. Thutmose carried out significant extensions to the temple of Amun-Ra at Karnak, including a columned hall, numerous colossal statues and a pair of obelisks.

Thutmose I was the first ruler to be buried in the Valley of the Kings, in a secret tomb prepared by the architect Ineni. The king's mummy has not yet been identified, though a coffin made for him was found in the 21st Dynasty cache at Deir el-Bahari. The body inside was too young to belong to Thutmose. The coffin was re-used for the 21st Dynasty king Pinodjem I.

Head of Thutmose I from one of his colossal statues in Karnak.

Hatshepsut (1473-1458 BC)

Hatshepsut, a daughter of Thutmose I, was the half-sister and principal wife of king Thutmose II. After his death, she became regent for her stepson Thutmose III.

Unlike other regents before her, Hatshepsut had herself crowned king. Texts and images present her as a male pharaoh. Thutmose III was pushed to the background. The most famous trade expedition in her reign went to the land of Punt (around Eritrea). This is recorded in Hatshepsut's terraced mortuary temple at Deir el-Bahari. The temple of Amun-Ra in Karnak received a new barque sanctuary and two pairs of enormous obelisks.

One of Hatshepsut's obelisks at Karnak. In the foreground is an obelisk of her father Thutmose I.

Hatshepsut had two tombs prepared for herself. The first was carved out in a valley south of Deir el-Bahari, while she was still a queen. It was left unfinished and replaced by a tomb in the Valley of the Kings. It is uncertain where Hatshepsut was buried. Her mummy has not been found or identified. Late in the reign of Thutmose III, all memory and representations of her were destroyed. Later king lists do not mention her.

Gold finger-ring with Hatshepsut's throne-name carved on a scarab.

Thutmose III (1479-1425 BC)

Thutmose III was a child when he inherited the crown. His step-mother Hatshepsut first acted as regent, then ruled as 'king' in her own right. Only after twenty years did Thutmose become sole ruler.

On Hatshepsut's death, Thutmose III launched a long series of campaigns in Syria-Palestine. He won a decisive victory at Megiddo and eventually he also took the city of Qadesh, which had led a rebellion against him. Thutmose also defeated Mitanni, across the river Euphrates. (He had the Egyptian fleet carried overland to the Euphrates by ox-carts.) In Nubia, too, Thutmose III secured the empire's border established by Thutmose I.

Head of a statue of Thutmose III from Karnak.

He built many temples. Karnak received seven new obelisks, two pylons (gateways), many halls and chapels, and the sacred lake. In the last decade of Thutmose's long reign, Hatshepsut's names and images were erased from her monuments.

Thutmose III was buried in the Valley of the Kings. His mummy was found in the 21st Dynasty cache at Deir el-Bahari. Thutmose III was long remembered as a hero and protective amulets were inscribed with his name.

Ring with a bezel showing Thutmose III as a sphinx.

Amenhotep II (1427-1400 BC)

Thutmose's son Amenhotep II became the next king, starting his rule as co-regent beside his father.

Amenhotep led three campaigns into Syria-Palestine, where some of Egypt's vassals rebelled. These campaigns showed that the new pharaoh was as strong as their previous ruler. Amenhotep displayed the corpses of seven Syrian chieftains he had killed by hanging them upside down from the prow of his ship. Six of the corpses were then hung up in front of the walls of Thebes, and the seventh was treated likewise in Nubia's capital Napata. The rulers of Mitanni, Babylon and the Hittites (in Anatolia) sent gifts in recognition of Egypt's power.

Amenhotep had himself presented as a great athlete with superhuman strength, who would row his own ship without help. He is depicted perfecting his archery skills, his arrows piercing thick plates of copper while he speeds by on a chariot pulled by galloping horses.

The mummy of Amenhotep II was found in his own tomb, still lying in his sarcophagus. In the 21st Dynasty, his tomb was employed as the last resting-place for eight additional pharaohs (including his two immediate successors), three ladies and a boy – transferred there from their own tombs for protection.

Shabti of Amenhotep II, from his tomb in the Valley of the Kings.

Thutmose IV (1400–1390 BC)

Thutmose IV, when still a prince, went out hunting in the desert at Giza. The son of Amenhotep II took a break in the shadow of the Great Sphinx of Khafra. The statue, now taken for an image of the sun-god Horemakhet, was buried deep in the sand.

According to a stela put up between the sphinx's paws, Thutmose had a dream in which the sphinx offered him the throne of Egypt if he would free the god from the encroaching dunes. We read, of course, that the prince took immediate action, and soon enough the prince was crowned king. Apparently Thutmose had not been the obvious heir from the outset, and the story was meant to prove that he had a divine right to the throne.

In the Near East, Egypt gradually lost territory to Mitanni, but a peace treaty was signed and the ruler of Mitanni sent Thutmose a daughter in marriage. In Nubia, the pharaoh crushed a rebellion.

Thutmose only rested in his tomb in the Valley of the Kings for some 350 years. His body was then moved to the tomb of his father with several other royal mummies, where it remained undisturbed until its modern discovery.

Bronze figure of Thutmose IV. The king brings a drink offering.

Amenhotep III & Tiye (1390–1352 BC)

Amenhotep III *Tiye*

The reign of this couple was Egypt's golden age. The country's wealth was unequalled at any other time.

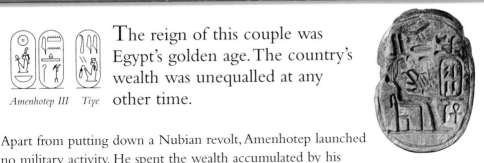

Scarab with an image of queen Tiye.

Apart from putting down a Nubian revolt, Amenhotep launched no military activity. He spent the wealth accumulated by his predecessors on temples and statues of a huge scale, only to be rivalled by Ramesses II. Art and architecture were of the finest quality. Many new temples appeared both in Egypt and Nubia. On the Theban West Bank, Amenhotep created new palaces and an artificial lake for use in his jubilee festivals. Of his vast mortuary temple, almost nothing remains but the 'Colossi of Memnon' – two huge statues of the king. Another colossal statue from here shows Amenhotep and Tiye enthroned together on the same scale. Clearly the queen enjoyed great authority, despite her non-royal descent. Both king and queen were deified during their lifetime. Tiye retained her prominent position in the reign of her son Akhenaten.

Amenhotep was buried in a valley to the west of the Valley of the Kings. Tiye's original burial place is not certain.

Colossal statue of Amenhotep III from his mortuary temple.

Akhenaten & Nefertiti (1352-1336 BC)

Akhenaten *Nefertiti*

The next king was a son of Amenhotep III and queen Tiye named Amenhotep. Nefertiti was his principal queen. Amenhotep IV soon changed his name ('Amun is satisfied') to Akhenaten ('Beneficial to Aten').

Gold ring with the throne-name of Akhenaten.

The new king worshipped only the sun-god as seen in the sky: the sun disc Aten. He built a large temple for Aten at Karnak, with wall-reliefs and colossal statues in a radical new style. Akhenaten then moved his court from Thebes to a new city called Akhetaten ('Horizon of Aten'), built in record time near modern Amarna. His reign is now called the 'Amarna Period'. The city had grand palaces and spacious houses for those who followed the royal family. Two large roofless temples were filled with numerous altars on which Aten's rays shone directly. Akhenaten banned the worship of the old gods, Amun above all. He had their names and images destroyed throughout Egypt and Nubia. A great hymn to Aten was

Akhenaten under the rays (with hands) of Aten. The sun disc itself is now missing. Originally this stela showed also Nefertiti and several daughters.

perhaps composed by the king himself, celebrating the god's creation and Akhenaten's role as his agent on earth. Monuments feature Nefertiti almost as prominently as her husband; this was unprecedented in Egypt.

Akhenaten vowed never to leave his capital, dedicating his life to his god. The new religion took some root among the elite surrounding the king, but the populace at large held on to their original beliefs. Akhenaten's radical

Fragment of a relief showing Nefertiti offering papyrus to Aten.

policies made him many enemies among Egypt's powerful families, who lost much of their influence under the new religion. The cult of Aten did not last after Akhenaten's death. Akhenaten was laid to rest – not for long – in a family tomb east of his capital. He was briefly succeeded by the enigmatic Smenkhkara, who some believe was really Nefertiti assuming the role of 'king'.

Later generations persecuted Akhenaten's memory – the king came to be recalled as 'the heretic'. His and Nefertiti's names and images were destroyed. Aten's temples and Akhetaten were quarried down and the blocks recycled in temples for the gods he had tried to banish. The Amarna Period was wiped out of history.

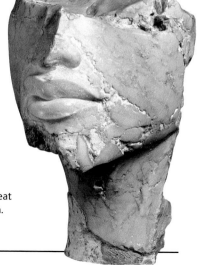

Fragment of a statue of Akhenaten. It once stood in the Great Temple of Aten in Amarna, but was smashed after his death.

Tutankhamun (1336–1327 BC)

 Nefertiti and Akhenaten had six daughters but no sons. Tutankhamun was probably the son of Akhenaten and a second wife named Kiya. When he came to the throne he was only about eight.

The king's original name was Tutankhaten ('Living image of Aten'). He changed it to Tutankhamun, because he brought back the old religion with Amun as the supreme god. His queen Ankhesenamen (originally Ankhesenpaaten) was a half-sister. The royal court abandoned Akhetaten for Memphis. A royal decree confirms his policy of restoring the old temples and reviving the old religion. The boy-king was largely a pawn in the hands of the regent Ay (perhaps Nefertiti's father) and general Horemheb. He had to distance himself from his Amarna predecessors.

Tutankhamun was about 20 when he died, perhaps murdered. He was briefly succeeded by Ay. Both were later wiped out of the historical record for their close association with the Amarna heresy. Ironically, Tutankhamun is now one of the best-known pharaohs, owing to the discovery in 1922 of his almost intact tomb in the Valley of the Kings.

Statue of Tutankhamun, later appropriated by Horemheb.

Horemheb (1323-1295 BC)

After Tutankhamun's death and the short reign of Ay, a general called Horemheb became pharaoh. The 18th Dynasty had ended.

Horemheb probably started his military career under Akhenaten. He became a powerful general under Tutankhamun. He led campaigns in Nubia and in Syria-Palestine, where Egypt's possessions were threatened by the rise of the Hittites. A large tomb was prepared for him in the necropolis of Saqqara at Memphis. But when Horemheb became king, he began a new tomb in the Valley of the Kings at Thebes. His queen Mutnodjmet was buried in the Saqqara tomb, and not in the Valley of the Queens.

Horemheb began to demolish Akhenaten's temples. He reused their blocks for new construction, such as three large pylons (gateways) in the temple of Amun-Ra at Karnak. He also had a rock-temple carved at Gebel el-Silsila. He usurped numerous monuments of Tutankhamun and Ay. When Horemheb died, his appointed heir, another general, came briefly to the throne as Ramesses I.

Pilaster from Horemheb's tomb at Saqqara. He is wearing the elaborate costume of a courtier, but a royal cobra was added to his forehead when he became pharaoh.

Sety I (1294-1279 BC)

After the short reign of Ramesses I, his son Sety inherited the throne. Sety's military campaigns restored Egypt's authority in Syria–Palestine.

Sety reconquered various former Egyptian possessions in Syria, including the strategic town of Qadesh, but later withdrew further south. Sety defeated the Libyans, who threatened the western Delta. He crushed an uprising in Nubia. Spectacular reliefs in the temple at Karnak recount his military successes. He began building the Great Hypostyle Hall at Karnak. In Abydos the king constructed a temple for Osiris and Egypt's other principal deities. Sety completed his predecessors' restoration work in the temples damaged during the Amarna Period.

Sety's mortuary temple on the Theban West Bank includes a chapel for his father Ramesses I. Sety's tomb is the longest in the Valley of the Kings and especially famous for its astronomical ceiling. His sarcophagus is now in London, in the John Soane's Museum. His mummy, found in the cache at Deir el–Bahari, is one of the best-preserved.

A *shabti* (tomb figure) of king Sety I from his tomb in Thebes.

36

Ramesses II (1279-1213 BC)

 Sety's son Ramesses II appears to have started his rule as his father's co-regent. He reigned for 67 years and became one of the most famous of all pharaohs.

In the Near East, Ramesses fought his famous battle against the Hittites at Qadesh. He narrowly escaped disaster after his regiment was ambushed by enemy forces. In his greatest temples, he commemorated the battle in prose and poetry. Ramesses presented it as a great victory, owing to his personal courage and his protection by Amun-Ra. In fact, the battle produced no clear victor, and the two powers later signed a peace treaty. This was sealed by Ramesses' marriage to two Hittite princesses. Letters from Ramesses to the Hittites have survived.

In the eastern Delta, Ramesses II founded the harbour-town Piramesse, close to a palace constructed by Sety I. It included large palaces, temples and statues of the king, some of which received worship as if he were a god. From then on, all the New Kingdom pharaohs resided in Piramesse.

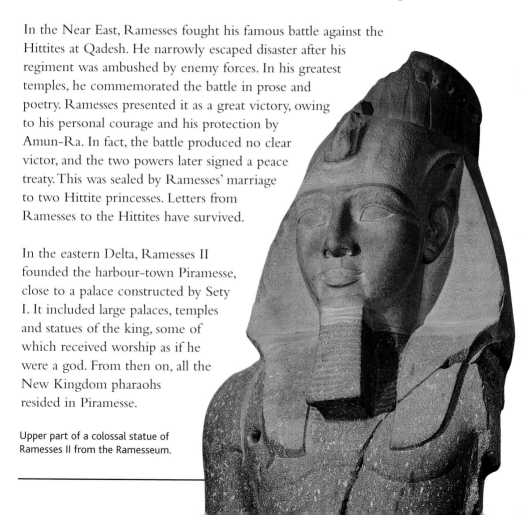

Upper part of a colossal statue of Ramesses II from the Ramesseum.

Ramesses II (Continued)

Ramesses II built more temples and had more statues carved of himself than any other pharaoh. He also took over monuments that had been made for previous kings. In Abydos he completed his father's temple and built another. In Nubia he created six rock-cut temples, the most famous of which are the two at Abu Simbel. In Thebes, he made important additions to the temples of Amun-Ra in Luxor and Karnak. Ramesses decorated the Great Hypostyle Hall in Karnak that had been begun by his father. On the West Bank he built a mortuary temple known as the Ramesseum. In it he erected the largest free-standing statue ever made in Egypt; it was destroyed in the Coptic Period, but important remains can still be seen today. His large tomb in the Valley of the Kings is now badly water-damaged, but his mummy was found among those later reburied in the cache at Deir el-Bahari.

The Great Hypostyle Hall at Karnak.

Nefertari (1279-1213 BC)

Statue of queen Nefertari.

 Nefertari was Ramesses II's principal wife during at least the first twenty years of his reign.

In many ways, Nefertari resembled Tiye, the wife of Amenhotep III – just as Ramesses mimicked Amenhotep's grandeur. Like Tiye, Nefertari was deified during her lifetime. Ramesses dedicated to her a magnificent rock-cut temple in Abu Simbel, in which she is likened to Hathor, the goddess of love and joy. Statues in the temple's façade represent the queen on the same colossal scale as her husband. In statues of Ramesses found elsewhere in Egypt, she is often represented beside his legs, on a smaller scale. Nefertari was a witness when the peace treaty of Qadesh was signed, and like her husband she engaged in correspondence with the Hittites.

When Nefertari died, her daughter Meritamun succeeded her as Ramesses' principal wife. Nefertari was buried in the largest, most beautiful tomb in the Valley of the Queens at Thebes. Its exquisite paintings have been restored in recent years. Her mummy has not survived.

One of the colossal statues of Nefertari at her temple in Abu Simbel.

Merenptah (1213–1203 BC)

Ramesses II outlived his twelve oldest sons. His thirteenth son, Merenptah, must have been in his fifties when he eventually succeeded his father.

During his brief reign, Merenptah had to deal with attacks from the Libyans and the 'Sea Peoples', a huge confederation of migrating peoples from the eastern Mediterranean. The invaders hoped to settle down in the Delta, but Merenptah defeated them. His most famous account of these events is the so-called Israel Stela. This bears the earliest mention of the people of Israel among Merenptah's opponents.

Merenptah's best-known monuments are a palace in Memphis and his tomb in the Valley of the Kings. The blocks and statues in Merenptah's mortuary temple were largely obtained from the nearby mortuary temple of Amenhotep III, which had been badly damaged by an earthquake. Merenptah's mummy was found reburied in the tomb of Amenhotep II.

The next king was Merenptah's son Sety II, whose throne was briefly contested by a usurper. Soon after, the 19th Dynasty came to an end with the sole rule of Tausret, Sety II's widow and initially regent for king Siptah.

Fragment of the calcite sarcophagus of Merenptah.

Ramesses III (1184–1153 BC)

The founder of the 20th Dynasty was Sethnakhte, who ruled briefly. His son Ramesses III succeeded him as the last important king of the New Kingdom.

Ramesses III's names and titles copy those of his great model, Ramesses II. He deliberately imitated that king in many other ways. His mortuary temple at Medinet Habu very closely resembles that of Ramesses II (the Ramesseum). His buildings on the sacred precinct of Amun-Ra in Karnak include a sanctuary for Amun's son Khons, a moon god.

Ramesses fought two important wars against the Libyans. He also had to defend Egypt against a new wave of the Sea Peoples, who had already attacked Egypt under Merenptah. Now they formed an even more formidable force, approaching in ships and over land via Syria. Ramesses' forces managed to destroy their fleet, which reached the Delta, and their troops in Palestine.

Ramesses was buried in the Valley of the Kings and his mummy was found in the Deir el-Bahari cache.

Ramesses III with the gods of Memphis: Ptah, Sekhmet and Nefertem.

The Last Ramessides (1153–1069 BC)

Ramesses VI   *Ramesses IX*

Ramesses III was succeeded by eight descendants who all took the name Ramesses.

Face of the sarcophagus of Ramesses VI.

There was strife within the family. Already under Ramesses III there had been a conspiracy to claim the throne for a minor prince, but Ramesses IV succeeded him as the legitimate heir. This king had great ambitions to prove himself worthy of his name, but he died too soon even to finish the grand scheme for his mortuary temple.

Ramesses V ruled even more briefly, and his tomb was usurped and expanded by Ramesses VI. Kings came and went, of whom Ramesses VI and IX appear to have been the last with any authority. Economic problems and civic unrest plagued the country. The enormous wealth accumulated by the temples of Amun–Ra in Thebes gave its high priests so much power that they effectively ruled Upper Egypt by themselves. Under Ramesses XI, the administration of Egypt became divided between a general Herihor, who became High Priest in Thebes, and a man called Smendes based in the Delta. Ramesses himself had become a background figure. Herihor even adopted royal titles and cartouches – a sure sign that the country was falling apart.

Sketch on an ostracon representing Ramesses IX receiving the crown prince (perhaps the later Ramesses X) and a vizier.

21st Dynasty (1069–945 BC)

Psusennes I

After Ramesses XI died, the official new king of Egypt was Smendes, the founder of the 21st Dynasty.

The 21st Dynasty did not rule from Piramesse but from Tanis, another Delta city. Many monuments were moved from the old to the new capital, and the new kings added their names to them. They built very little of their own, so we know little about them. The best-known king is Psusennes I, Smendes' successor. His unplundered tomb was discovered in Tanis. It contained the best preserved royal burial after that of Tutankhamun. Several other intact royal burials were found within the same temple.

The high priests in Thebes continued to rule over almost the whole of Upper Egypt. The two lines of rulers appear to have coexisted peacefully and intermarried. Psusennes I was, in fact, the son of a Theban High Priest. Both in the north and the south, an increasingly powerful segment of the population was formed by Libyan descendants of war captives from the late New Kingdom, who had been forcibly settled in colonies within Egypt. One king of the 21st Dynasty, Osorkon I, was actually a Libyan.

Lintel with an official showing respect to the names of Siamun, a king of the 21st Dynasty.

22nd–24th Dynasties (945–715 BC)

Sheshonq I   *Osorkon II*

The next dynasty in Tanis was formed by a family of Libyans, the first king being Sheshonq I.

Sheshonq gained an important victory against the kingdoms of Israel and Judah, thereby re-establishing Egyptian influence in Palestine. His victories are recounted on his monuments in Thebes – the first major construction work for a long time. The family of high priests who had been ruling from Thebes had died out, so Sheshonq installed a son of his own as their successor. He thus gained some control of the entire land. Major building activity under his successor, Osorkon II, is further evidence that the country's economy had improved.

But during the mid-22nd Dynasty, there was a Theban rebellion against another Tanite prince who had been installed there as High Priest. A civil war erupted, and the country rapidly fell apart into several smaller kingdoms, simultaneously ruled by the 22nd to 24th Dynasties and various other minor princes. This internal weakness made Egypt an easy prey for a force looming outside Egypt's borders: the kingdom of Kush.

Temple relief from Bubastis showing king Osorkon II and his wife Karomama.

25th Dynasty (747–656 BC)

Piankhy   *Taharqa*

At the end of the Third Intermediate Period, the kingdom of Kush was a re-emerging power in Nubia. One Kushite king, Piankhy, even conquered Egypt.

His successor Shabaqa consolidated control over Lower Egypt. The Kushites who ruled both Kush and Egypt are known as the '25th Dynasty'. They displayed their reverence for the Egyptian religion, especially for Amun, whom they had come to worship at home. They fostered an artistic revival looking back at Egypt's past. The Nubian kings built temples with colossal statues and were even buried under pyramids, the greatest builder being Taharqa. He withstood an Assyrian invasion attempt but had to flee a second, when Memphis was taken. A third Assyrian attack pushed him back for good. The Delta princes who had fought alongside him were killed apart from Nekau I of Sais and his son Psamtek I, whom the Assyrians used to enforce their control. In a spectacular campaign Taharqa's successor Tanutamani briefly reconquered the whole of Egypt, killing Nekau. But a fourth Assyrian invasion brought Kush's rule of Egypt to an end.

Statue of king Taharqa, protected by the ram of Amun, from his temple at Kawa in Nubia.

26th Dynasty (664–525 BC)

Psamtek I   *Amasis*

The Assyrians installed Psamtek I to rule Egypt for them. He eventually took control of all Egypt and founded the 26th Dynasty.

Psamtek brought prosperity. The art and religious customs of Egypt's great past were carefully copied. His successor Nekau II conquered Israel and Judah, but the rising power of Babylon soon forced him to abandon his claims. Psamtek II sent his armies south into the heartland of Kush, crushing their ambitions to reconquer Egypt. At home he persecuted the memory of the Kushite 25th-Dynasty kings.

The next king, Apries, was deposed by his own troops after a disastrous campaign against Greek colonisers on the Libyan coast. General Amasis seized the crown. To curb the power of Babylon and then Persia, Amasis pursued a careful policy of varying alliances and military intervention. In these days, the pharaohs depended heavily on Greek and Carian mercenaries.

Only six months into his reign, Amasis' son and successor Psamtek III died in an invasion by king Cambyses of Persia. For some 121 years, Egypt became a satrapy of the Persian empire (the '27th Dynasty').

Basalt relief from a temple of Psamtek I in the Delta. The king's facial features are represented in a highly realistic fashion, perhaps as a rare instance of attempted portraiture.

25th – 30th Dynasties (404-343 BC)

Nectanebo I   Nectanebo II

Between 404 and 400 BC, Egypt was liberated from Persian rule by Amyrtaios, sole king of the '28th Dynasty' from Sais.

The throne was then seized by the 29th Dynasty from Mendes, another Delta town. King Hakoris foiled a Persian attempt to reconquer Egypt. Another usurper, general Nectanebo (I), founded the 30th Dynasty. His prolific building activity reflects Egypt's prosperity. Artistic production reached the same levels as during the 26th Dynasty. Nectanebo I fought off a new Persian invasion and entered an alliance with Sparta and Athens.

The next king was Teos, but his brother claimed the crown for his son Nectanebo II while Teos was away campaigning in Syria-Palestine. The army supported the new king and Teos fled to Persia. There were two more Persian attacks on Egypt, and the second restored Egypt to the Persian empire. Nectanebo II, the last native pharaoh, fled and was never buried in the sarcophagus that had been prepared for him (now in the British Museum). Persian rule finally ended when Alexander the Great of Macedonia took Egypt in 332 BC.

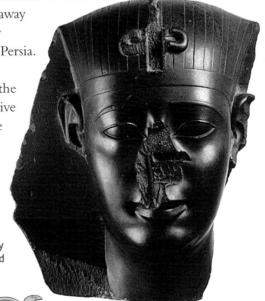

This head of a royal statue, most probably of Nectanebo I, shows the highly idealised style that prevailed in the art of his days.

The Ptolemies (332-30 BC)

Alexander *Ptolemy I* *Cleopatra VII*

Alexander the Great conquered Egypt without resistance. He was crowned pharaoh in Memphis. The oracle in Siwa Oasis hailed him as the son of the god Amun. He founded a new capital: Alexandria.

After Alexander's death, his general Ptolemy proclaimed himself king of Egypt, founding the dynasty of the Ptolemies. Fourteen kings and a series of queens (mostly co-regents) succeeded him. They built temples to the Egyptian gods, but there were uprisings against them. Economic problems and family conflicts further weakened the Ptolemies. Rome became the new dominant power in the last century BC, and the Ptolemies grew dependent on Roman support.

Cleopatra VII, the last Ptolemaic ruler, increased her power through unions with Julius Caesar and then Mark Antony, but finally Rome, led by Octavian, went to war with the couple. Egypt lost the Battle of Actium (30 BC), and became a Roman province. Cleopatra and Antony committed suicide. Pharaonic culture lasted another few centuries but was gradually marginalised by the rise of Christianity. In AD 535, emperor Justinian closed the last Egyptian temple.

Stela with Ptolemy II as a pharaoh bringing offerings to the sacred bull of Armant. The Ptolemies were Greek, but they sustained and copied Egyptian traditions.